Brief Notes

FINANCE

The publications in *Brief Notes* are outlines of core topics of interest to professionals involved in shopping center management. The outlines are capsule overviews of each topic. Many key points are covered, and shopping center examples are provided for further illustration. Core concepts in each area guide you on topics you may want to explore further. Each outline also contains a helpful glossary.

Brief Notes is designed to provide a helpful and informative overview of the topics covered. It is not intended to be a substitute for more extensive learning that can be achieved through attending ICSC educational programs and reading additional ICSC professional publications.

The outlines contained in *Brief Notes: Shopping Center Management:*

- Management Overview
- Finance
- Insurance and Risk Management
- The Lease and Its Language
- Leasing Strategies
- Maintenance
- Marketing
- Retailing
- Security

Brief Notes

FINANCE

International Council of Shopping Centers
New York

ABOUT THE INTERNATIONAL COUNCIL OF SHOPPING CENTERS

The International Council of Shopping Centers (ICSC) is the trade association of the shopping center industry. Serving the shopping center industry since 1957, ICSC is a not-for-profit organization with over 44,000 members in 77 countries worldwide.

ICSC members include shopping center

- owners
- developers
- managers
- marketing specialists
- leasing agents
- retailers
- researchers
- attorneys

- architects
- contractors
- consultants
- investors
- lenders and brokers
- academics
- public officials

ICSC sponsors more than 200 meetings a year and provides a wide array of services and products for shopping center professionals, including deal making events, conferences, educational programs, accreditation, awards, publications and research data.

For more information about ICSC, write or call the
International Council of Shopping Centers
1221 Avenue of the Americas
New York, NY 10020-1099
Telephone: 646-728-3800
Fax: 212-589-5555
info@icsc.org
http://www.icsc.org

This publication is designed to provide accurate and authoritative information in regard to the subject matter covered. It is sold with the understanding that the publisher is not engaged in rendering legal, accounting, or other professional services. If legal advice or other expert assistance is required, the services of a competent professional person should be sought.

> —*From a Declaration of Principles jointly adopted by a Committee of the American Bar Association and a Committee of Publishers.*

Companies, professional groups, clubs and other organizations may qualify for special terms when ordering quantities of more than 20 of this title.

Published by
International Council of Shopping Centers
Publications Department
1221 Avenue of the Americas
New York, NY 10020-1099

ICSC Catalog No.: 242

ISBN: 1-58268-028-0

Contents

Preface

The job of shopping center managers is to maximize the center's net operating income (NOI) and the value of their shopping centers. To do this, managers must understand what value means, the forces that affect it (especially those the manager can control), and the ways it is determined. Managers must also understand how the financial information derived from the budgeting process can be used as tools to enhance value.

The task is not as formidable as it may seem. The following pages explain the key points that will help you—the shopping center professional—understand value and how to increase it. Numerous examples take you step by step through the various financial analyses you must be able to perform. Key words, terms and concepts are clearly defined in the text and also appear in the accompanying glossary.

Acknowledgments

The material in this outline is based in part on a course presented at the International Council of Shopping Centers (ICSC) John T. Riordan School for Professional Development Management Institute.

The International Council of Shopping Centers gratefully acknowledges the individuals mentioned below, who have contributed their expertise to this publication.

Paul G. Dasso, CSM/CPM
Robert J. Flynn, CSM
Mary Kate Herron, Vice President, Lease Management, Heritage Property Investment Trust, Inc.

THE CONCEPT OF VALUE

Simply stated, value is the price an informed buyer is willing to pay for a shopping center on the open market. The value is based on the net operating income (NOI) the center generates (along with other factors), rather than on the value of the physical aspects of the building and underlying land. When viewing the value of a shopping center, an owner and seller typically consider the annual net operating income (NOI) and divide it by an agreed capitalization rate to arrive at the value. The lower the capitalization rate, the higher the value.

Forces That Affect Value

Numerous external factors are constantly influencing the value of a given real estate property. The factors typically influence the agreed capitalization rate (cap rate) to be lower or higher. Among these are:

- Social forces, including:

    —Population growth and decline
    —Shifts in population density and composition
    —Employment and leisure trends
    —Attitudes toward education and technology

- Economic forces, including:

    —Area competition and new development
    —Commercial and industrial trends
    —Employment and salary trends
    —Availability of money and credit
    —Price levels, interest rates, and tax burdens

- Political forces, including:

    —Zoning laws
    —Building codes
    —Police and fire regulations
    —Government housing
    —Monetary policies

- Physical forces, including:

    —Climate and topography
    —Transportation infrastructure
    —Community factors (schools, parks)
    —Environmental considerations.

Certain basic principles of real property value also come into play, such as supply and demand; competition anticipation; and optimum use of the property, or highest and best use—the use that will yield the most profitable return.

Other financial factors that affect cap rates used to determine value include:

- Risk and the perception of risk:
    - Safety of the investment (an established shopping center is safer than a high tech startup, but not as safe as a Treasury bill)
    - Certainty of yield (the yield will depend on the cash flow, which will depend on tenant viability)
    - Liquidity (shopping centers, particularly large centers have low liquidity, while shares in a large publicly traded shopping center REIT have high liquidity)
    - Marketability (this will vary, depending on the return an investor can get from other investments at a given point)
    - Collateral value of the property (few lenders will lend more than 70% of the value of a center)
    - Acceptable duration (How long will the money be tied up?)
    - Freedom from care (shopping centers require time, skill, and management attention, this is really an adjustment for effort)
    - Potential for appreciation/depreciation (One man's lemon is another's lemonade! Most real estate is purchased with the assumption the new owner can add value through leasing of vacant space and expiring leases at higher rents, more efficient management and improved marketing results).

- Leverage: The use of borrowed funds for investment. The higher the proportion of borrowed funds, the higher the leverage and the lower the proportion of equity funds. Loan-to-value ratio varies according to real estate investment trends, the condition of the debt market and other cyclical financing trends.

- Equity: The value of the owner's interest in the property in excess of all claims and liens. (The same concept as the equity you would have if you owned your home!)

The Time Value of Money

From an investor's perspective, the earning power of a shopping center is the critical element affecting its value: the higher the anticipated earnings, the higher the value. Thus, investment in an income-producing shopping center property represents the exchange of present dollars for the right to receive future dollars.

Because economic and social forces are constantly modifying property value, anyone contemplating investing in a property, or anyone appraising (valuing) it, must always view it as subject to change. It is often difficult to predict the long-term viability of a tenant. With most national retailers' performance widely reported because they are publicly traded companies, analysts are constantly assessing the retailers' viability. One quarter your anchor tenant may be the darling of Wall Street, and the next Wall Street analysts may be announcing "strong sell" (of their stock) ratings. Also, the competitive climate causes retailers to operate on razor-thin margins that stand between profit and loss. A few quarters of losses can send a large retail chain heading for protection under federal bankruptcy laws. This results in rent restructuring and massive store closings. It is always wise to be aware of the financial condition of your tenants, as your cash flow (and subsequently your center value) can change quickly.

Value at a given time represents the monetary worth of a property to buyers and sellers. An important factor is the time value of money, the concept underlying compound interest: that a dollar received today is worth more than a dollar in the future, due to opportunity cost, inflation, and certainty of payment.

An owner's specific rights in an income-producing shopping center include the right to receive all profits accruing to it during the period of ownership plus the reversionary value: the proceeds from resale at the end of the investment period. Important considerations in understanding both present and future value include:

- Simple and compound interest rates
- Compounding
- Discounting

A ten-year period of ownership is a comparable measurement for a financial model.

Interest Rates

Interest is a sum paid or calculated for the use of capital (the renting of money). It is usually expressed as a rate or percentage of the capital. In its simplest terms, it is the same as a home mortgage finance charge or income on a savings account.

Compound Interest

Compound interest is the interest on interest; interest earned during a given period is added to the principal and included in the next period's interest calculation. Over time it can make a significant contribution. Understanding compound interest can help people calculate the return on savings and investments, as well as the cost of borrowing.

Discounting

Because income in an unpredictable future is worth less than money in hand now, future income must be discounted—converted into its present value. Future income is further eroded by inflation. The discount rate used (which is usually derived from the financial market) reflects the compensation necessary to persuade an investor or lender to give up liquidity, to wait or to defer consumption, and to assume the risks of investing. It is the rate of return on an investment. It does not include any provision for recovering the capital invested. In appraisal analysis, "discount rate" means the same as "interest rate," but the term emphasizes the fact that future income receipts are being capitalized—valued in today's dollars. (Capitalization is discussed below.)

A discount rate is based on the assumption that investors must seek compensation for bearing risk (inflation/reduced purchasing power/sacrificing liquidity), and forgoing the current use of capital. The discount rate is the summation of the compensation for all these factors. Much of this is already "priced" in the form of a ten-year Treasury note, the benchmark for a safe rate of return. The higher the discount rate, the higher the risk assumed.

Compound Interest Tables

These printed tables (often now found programmed into financial calculator software) are used to calculate past, present, and future values over a period of years. For example, if a lease stipulates that the unit charge for common area expenses will be increased every year at a particular percentage over the previous year's charge, compound interest tables help compute what the charge will be in five years and what it was five years ago. The tables (see sample table) are printed for various interest rates and periods—monthly, quarterly, or annually. They are set up in six columns. The first three indicate future values:

1. **The amount of 1 at compound interest:** The future worth of $1 with interest, or how much $1 put in the bank today at a given rate of interest will grow in a given number (n) of periods

2. **The accumulation of $1 per period:** The future worth of $1 per period with interest—in other words, the sum that would accumulate over n periods at a given rate of interest if $1 was deposited at the end of each period

3. **The sinking fund factor:** The amount that must be deposited at the end of the period, and at the end of each period thereafter, to accumulate $1, including interest, in a given number of periods at a given rate of interest. For example, it would show how much to put in reserve in a bank today and at the end of each year to have enough money to repaint a center's canopies n years from now.

The next three columns reflect present values of money:

4. **The present value reversion of 1:** The present worth of the right to receive $1 in n periods at a given rate of interest—how much to pay today to get $1 at some time in the future

5. **The present value of an ordinary annuity of 1 per period:** The present worth of the right to receive $1 at the end of each period for n periods at a given rate of interest—how much to pay today for the right to receive an income stream over time

6. The installment to amortize 1 (mortgage amortization table): The amount of the periodic installments that must be paid to pay off $1, including principal and interest, over n periods at a given rate of interest.

ANNUAL COMPOUND INTEREST AND ANNUITY 10.00%

	Amount Of 1	Amount Of 1 Per Period	Sinking Fund Payment	Present Worth Of 1	Present Worth of 1 Per Period	Periodic Payment To Amortize 1
	What a single $1 deposit grows to in the future. The deposit is made at the beginning of the first period.	What a series of $1 deposits grow to in the future. A deposit is made at the end of each period.	The amount to be deposited at the end of each period that grows to $1 in the future.	What $1 to be paid in the future is worth today. Value today of a single $1 payment tomorrow.	What $1 to be paid at the end of each period is worth today. Value today of a series of $1 payments tomorrow.	The mortgage payment to amortize a loan of $1. An annuity certain, payable at the end of each period, worth $1 today.
	$S = (1 + i)^n$	$s_{\overline{n}} = \dfrac{(1 + i)^n - 1}{i}$	$\dfrac{1}{s_{\overline{n}}} = \dfrac{i}{(1 + i)^n - 1}$	$V^n = \dfrac{1}{(1 + i)^n}$	$a_{\overline{n}} = \dfrac{1 - V^n}{i}$	$\dfrac{1}{a_{\overline{n}}} = \dfrac{i}{1 - V^n}$
YEAR						
	1.100 000	1.000 000	1.000 000 0000	.909 091	.909 091	1.100 000 0000
1	1.100 000	1.000 000	1.000 000 0000	.909 091	.909 091	1.100 000 0000
2	1.210 000	2.100 000	.476 190 4762	.826 446	1.735 537	.576 190 4762
3	1.331 000	3.310 000	.302 114 8036	.751 315	2.486 852	.402 114 8036
4	1.464 100	4.641 000	.215 470 8037	.683 013	3.169 865	.315 470 8037
5	1.610 510	6.105 100	.163 797 4808	.620 921	3.790 787	.263 797 4808
6	1.771 561	7.715 610	.129 607 3804	.564 474	4.355 261	.229 607 3804
7	1.948 717	9.487 171	.105 405 4997	.513 158	4.868 419	.205 405 4997
8	2.143 589	11.435 888	.087 444 0176	.466 507	5.334 926	.187 444 0176
9	2.357 948	13.579 477	.073 640 5391	.424 098	5.759 024	.173 640 5391
10	2.593 742	15.937 425	.062 745 3949	.385 543	6.144 567	.162 745 3949
11	2.853 117	18.531 167	.053 963 1420	.350 494	6.495 061	.153 963 1420
12	3.138 428	21.384 284	.046 763 3151	.318 631	6.813 692	.146 763 3151
13	3.452 271	24.522 712	.040 778 5238	.289 664	7.103 356	.140 778 5238
14	3.797 498	27.974 983	.035 746 2232	.263 331	7.366 687	.135 746 2232
15	4.177 248	31.772 482	.031 473 7769	.239 392	7.606 080	.131 473 7769
16	4.594 973	35.949 730	.027 816 6207	.217 629	7.823 709	.127 816 6207
17	5.054 470	40.544 703	.024 664 1344	.197 845	8.012 553	.124 664 1344
18	5.559 917	45.599 173	.021 930 2222	.179 859	8.201 412	.121 930 2222
19	6.115 909	51.159 090	.019 546 8682	.163 508	8.364 920	.119 546 8682
20	6.727 500	57.274 999	.017 459 6248	.148 644	8.513 564	.117 459 6248
21	7.400 250	64.002 499	.015 624 3898	.135 131	8.648 694	.115 624 3898
22	8.140 275	71.402 749	.014 005 0630	.122 846	8.771 540	.114 005 0630
23	8.954 302	79.543 024	.012 571 8127	.111 678	8.883 218	.112 571 8127
24	9.849 733	88.497 327	.011 299 7764	.101 526	8.984 744	.111 299 7764
25	10.834 706	98.347 059	.010 168 0722	.092 296	9.077 040	.110 168 0722
26	11.918 177	109.181 765	.009 159 0386	.083 905	9.160 945	.109 159 0386
27	13.109 994	121.099 942	.008 257 6423	.076 278	9.237 223	.108 257 6423
28	14.420 994	134.209 936	.007 451 0132	.069 343	9.306 567	.107 451 0132
29	15.863 093	148.630 930	.006 728 0747	.063 039	9.369 606	.106 728 0747
30	17.449 402	164.494 023	.006 079 2483	.057 309	9.426 914	.106 079 2483

From David Thorndike, *Thorndike Encyclopedia of Banking and Financial Tables, 3rd Edition*. Copyright © by Warren, Gorham & Lamont, Inc. Reprinted by permission.

Core Concepts

✓ Replacement vs. market comps vs. income approach to value

✓ NOI, EBITDA, FFO

✓ $I \div R = V$

✓ The higher the cap rate (the higher the risk) the lower the value

DETERMINING THE VALUE OF A SHOPPING CENTER

E stablishing the value of a real estate property is important for many reasons, including obtaining financing, securitization, attracting buyers, adding joint venture partners or investors, apprising other investors in the venture, selling, evaluating real estate assessments for property tax purposes, evaluating insurance coverage, or simply measuring growth and returns on investment.

Value can be estimated in several ways. Traditional appraisal frequently involves a detailed report using these three approaches:

■ Reproduction cost, or replacement value: The amount it

would cost to reproduce a similar property, derived by estimating the value of the land if it were vacant and adding what it would cost to reproduce the improvements, less accrued depreciation. (Depreciation is a loss from the upper limit of value caused by age, deterioration and/or obsolescence. Accrued depreciation is the actual difference between the cost of replacement as new and the present value). This approach is probably less accurate for an older center, where depreciation becomes a major factor. An older center may be worth substantially less than the sum total of the land, buildings, and developer's entrepreneurship when using this approach without taking into consideration the value of the cash flow.

- Market sales comparison, or comparable value: This takes into account the amount for which a comparable property has recently sold. Typical units of comparison include sales price paid per square foot of the building area. However, this approach is often limited by a lack of precisely comparable market transactions.

- Income capitalization, or cash flow analysis: This method— the most common for valuing a shopping center income-producing asset—estimates the value of a property by calculating the present worth of the net income it could potentially produce during the remainder of its productive life, or some other period of time. One technique used to convert that future income into present value is capitalization (discussed below). The capitalized value is, in effect, the sum of the anticipated annual income less the loss of interest until the time of collection. This is generally the most reliable appraisal approach, but its reliability depends on the quality of estimates made and the derivation of capitalization rates. In the shopping center industry, this is the valuation technique that is most widely used.

The Income Approach—Net Cash Flow Analysis

Here are the basic steps in arriving at net operating income, taxable income, and net cash flow.

1. Determine gross receipts from shopping center operations less an appropriate vacancy and rent loss factor. A 5% vacancy factor is generally used in models, to account for tenant transitions. The gross receipts also include CAM and real estate taxes reimbursables, along with temporary tenant and vending income.
2. Deduct operating expenses. The result is net operating income (NOI). NOI is the line used in calculating a center's value. Earnings before interest, taxes, depreciation and amortization (EBITDA) is analogous to NOI, and is used by REITS to approximate the "cash-generating" power of a company before deductions for interest expense, payback of principle on loans, corporate taxes and depreciation.
3. Subtract the appropriate depreciation for the period and the interest portion of the debt service. The result is taxable income.
4. Subtract the income tax, based on the applicable tax rate of the taxpayer (shopping center owner). The result is income after taxes.
5. Deduct the amortization portion of the debt service. (This has been paid and is a cash item.)
6. Add the depreciation. (This is a non-cash item and was deducted for tax purposes in step 3.) The result is net cash flow. Funds from operations (FFO) is a form of modified

net cash flow with certain accounting adjustments used by REITs comparable to the bottom-line earnings of other businesses.

In brief:

Gross income
− Operating expenses
Net operating income

− Depreciation
− Interest
Taxable income

− Income tax
− Amortization
+ Depreciation
Net cash flow

The Income Approach—Capitalization into Value

It is possible to use the net operating income to arrive at a value for the shopping center. That is because real estate is a capital good, and benefits from owning it are received over a prolonged period of time. As discussed above, the value of a capital good is measured by calculating how much of the promise of future income is worth today (the present worth of the income anticipated over a specified time); the process is known as capitalization. **It determines the amount of money (capital sum) that would be paid in the open market to obtain the forecasted net income over the specified time.**

The figure used to convert income into value is the capitalization rate (cap rate). It is a percentage that is the sum of the discount rate and the capital recovery, or recapture rate (the rate of return on the investment plus the actual return of the investment). The figure does not include capital depreciation or debt service. The rate is market-driven and attained through negotiation. The higher the risk, the higher the cap rate, thus the lower the value. You must be careful in looking at NOI alone, as it does not reflect potential risks (center with a dark anchor), certainty of costs (center with no HVAC or lot reserve), or quality of income (center with shell corporations on many leases and a large number of local tenants). For example, a purchaser of a low-risk shopping center with excellent fundamentals and high-level certainty of income producing leases might be perfectly content to receive an 8 percent return on the net operating income, thus a cap rate of 8 percent might be agreed upon. If the NOI were $5 million, the value would be arrived as follows: $5,000,000 ÷ .08 = $62,500,000. Considerations involved in arriving at the rate may include:

- Competitive market conditions and alternative investment opportunities
- The capital market—defined as funds market—where buyers and sellers get together to trade various types of long-term instruments (long-term meaning a maturity date of more than one year), such as stocks, bonds, and mortgages
- The money market, involving various types of short-term investments, of one year or less. There is a general relationship between the money market and the capital market. Usually, the longer one has to wait to receive money, the more risk is assumed and the higher the interest rate or yield is expected to be, so long-term investments tend to offer higher rates or yields than short-term investments.

The formula for capitalizing income into value is:

Value = Net Operating Income ÷ Capitalization Rate

or

$$V = I \div R$$

Conversely, income divided by cap rate equals value, or

$$I \div R = V$$

As an exercise, capitalize into value a shopping center with the following statistics:

Size	100,000 sq. ft. of GLA
Land cost	$300,000
Building cost	$5,000,000
Gross income	$11/sq. ft.
Operating expenses	$3/sq. ft.
Capitalization rate	11.75%

Net operating income (gross income minus operating expenses) $1,100,000 − $300,000 = $800,000

Value $800,000 ÷ .1175 = $6,808,511

If, on the other hand, the center was considered to have a high risk, poor fundamentals and questionable income from its leases, a purchaser might negotiate with the seller a higher cap rate, perhaps as high as 12 percent return on the net operating income. If the NOI were $5 million, the value would be much different, as noted below:

$5,000,000 ÷ 12 = $41,666,667

Because the capitalization rate reflects market conditions and perceived risk, the value of the center will vary with the cap rate regardless of the net operating income.

Core Concepts

✓ Increasing income
✓ Decreasing expenses
✓ Increasing NOI
✓ Impacting value
✓ Gross leases, CAM caps

WHAT CAREFUL MANAGEMENT CAN DO TO AFFECT VALUE

Even a small adjustment to the income stream can have a significant effect on the property's value. For example, say a small shopping center's common area expenses total $78,600, while only $50,500 is recovered from tenants (a 64.2% CAM or recovery rate). Assume that the shortfall is due to unrealistic ceilings written into some leases, that those ceilings can be eliminated, and that the capitalization rate is 11%. That extra annual $28,100 divided by the 11% cap rate represents $255,455 improvement in the center's potential market value. NOI is impacted by either increasing income or decreasing expenses. If you are aware that the recovery rate is only 64%, you may choose to spread a landscaping project over 3 years, rather than doing it all in one year. This would be especially wise if a large tenant with a very low cap on CAM was being replaced in the next year.

Income Management

To determine how to achieve the greatest amount of income without damaging the property's future productivity, managers may evaluate aspects of the lease agreements such as:

- Lease term
- Tax and insurance responsibilities
- Offsets against overage rents
- Common area maintenance (CAM) costs
- Credit standing

Long-range lease clause possibilities also worth review include:

- Refined tax clauses for rent and other replacement taxes
- Refined advertising clauses
- Kickout (right to terminate) clauses
- Administrative surcharges
- Net-net-net leases

It is important to understand that non-financial lease provisions can significantly impact your cash flow. Never underestimate the usefulness of a complete lease abstract. A kickout clause, a percentage rent recap clause, a co-tenancy clause, or an exclusive clause violation can materially impact your rent cash flow.

Other areas for constant review might include:

- Awareness of competition

- The social, political, economic, and physical forces mentioned previously
- Placing more stress on a tenant's retailing ability, advertising and display techniques, and advertising philosophy. The income stream is only as strong as the source it is coming from.

Controlling Expenses

Income management encompasses not just calculating what tenants pay through minimum rent agreements, but also recovery of charges for center costs such as common area maintenance (discussed below) and real estate taxes.

Recovery of payments for expenses is an important area to examine, since center management may not recover all costs if leases contain limits on recovery. This is what was discussed above with recovery rates. This is a significant area, as leases are negotiated in different economic climates. Those negotiated in weaker economic times will usually have more "tenant-friendly" clauses, while those negotiated in a booming economy will be more inclined to have stronger landlord language. Also, some tenants and landlords prefer a "gross lease." In this type of lease, the landlord estimates the total cost of maintaining the shopping center and adds the pro-rata share of that specific tenant as a fixed CAM portion to the fixed minimum rent. Some items that vary significantly may be charged separately, like snow removal. This fixed CAM may have annual escalations tied to the consumer price index.

Examine the expense side of the budget, particularly real estate taxes, insurance, utilities, and labor, to determine how each might be handled better and at lower cost. Reducing expenses increases the net operating income. Since tenants can usually pay 10 to 12 percent of their sales in total occupancy costs, the lower the operating costs billed to the tenant, the higher rent it can pay in theory.

Core Concepts

✓ Analyzing operating reports and tenant sales reports

✓ Calculating minimum and percentage rents

✓ Breakpoints—natural and artificial

BUDGETING AS A MONITORING TOOL

Understanding the details of the budget forecast is one of the first steps in identifying opportunities to improve net operating income and enhance the property's value. Analyzing sales and rent levels can identify tenants with problems and indicate the need either to recapture the space or to offer assistance in return for a restructured lease that improves the income and value of the property. Tools to conduct a financial analysis of center operations and monitor tenants' performance may include:

- Operating reports:

    —Monthly operating report or profit and loss statement—the income and expenses for the period. The information may include the month's actual figures, the month's budget, the year-to-date budgeted and actual figures, variances in real dollars and in percentages, funds available to spend on annual budget, and the amount spent last year.

—Payroll, utilities, and other scheduled charges. It is useful if these charges are recorded within the period of the profit and loss statement.

—Balance sheet, cash flow statement, rent rolls, and accounts receivable.

■ Sales reports:

—Tenants' sales performance may be ranked in a variety of ways, listed in order of percentage sales variations by category, by monthly sales rank, or by sales per square foot. Comparing these figures to industry standards per category will indicate which areas are underperforming.

Remember, sales drive rent, rent drives NOI, and NOI drives value. Many landlords examine a tenant's health ratio (also called occupancy cost) annually to identify potential problems. This percentage ratio is usually (annual rent + annual real estate taxes + annual CAM + annual marketing fund contribution) divided by annual sales. It varies by category, but a good rule of thumb in identifying potential issues is over 10%.

Budgeting

The numbers a manager develops for a budget will be based on analysis of the center's past performance and on a plan of how to improve performance within a given set of conditions. For example, if a center's shoe business has been flat for several years, the budget would take into account how the center intends to help push those tenants back into overages (rent in addition to a stated minimum rent—see percentage rent, discussed below) and what the anticipated impact of those efforts will be.

Operational and financial goals are usually established on a property-by-property basis by ownership as part of the annual budgeting process. These are the guidelines you will use for the applicable period.

Other trends and conditions must also be considered in budget making, from economic forecasts to information about which leases will be expiring/vacating in the coming year.

Budgeting Rents

Rent rolls and sales records are the starting points for projecting rent. The features of the rent roll and sales reports may include:

- Each tenant's square footage
- Lease commencement and expiration dates
- Minimum rent
- The percentage rent rate and breakpoint
- Most recent 12-month sales
- Projected sales
- Change between this year's and last year's sales
- Estimated percentage rent to be paid this year

Minimum rent usually is the center's greatest source of revenue, but percentage rent is an important supplement to that basic rental income. Though percentage rent is the most volatile portion of income, it is the one on which management can have the most impact.

Temporary tenants are also a source of income. As an example, if you needed to add three electrical ground outlets and phone lines (total cost $500) and get an insurance binder for $500 to accommodate a temporary holiday tenant who was paying $250 a week for the 10 weeks prior to Christmas, what would be your ROI? ($2,500/$1,000 = 250%)

The necessary rate of return on investment (ROI: that required by the market or by a specific investor) is the capitalization rate, discussed above.

Calculating Minimum Rent

Calculation of minimum rent must take into account the targeted return on investment after covering the mortgage and other costs associated with debt. The following example shows how to calculate the required minimum guaranteed rent needed to cover the mortgage and other costs and meet the investor's targeted return on investment.

The developer-owner plans to add a 30,000-square-foot free-standing supermarket. The cost is $50 per square foot, and total operating costs are estimated at an additional $1.40 per square foot for real estate taxes and insurance. The developer can borrow 80% of the building costs at 8.5% interest for 23 years (a 9.92% mortgage constant), and wants a cash dividend (before depreciation and income taxes) of 12% on its equity in the building, exclusive of land.

Building cost:
30,000 sq. ft. × $50/sq. ft. = $1,500,000

The loan:

$1,500,000 × 80% = $1,200,000

Debt service (mortgage constant):

$1,200,000 × 9.92% = $119,040

Additional operating costs:

30,000 sq. ft. × $1.40/sq. ft. = $42,000

The developer's equity (building cost minus loan):

$1,500,000 − $1,200,000 = $300,000

The necessary ROI:

$300,000 × 12% = $36,000

Debt service + operating costs + ROI:

$119,040 + $42,000 + $36,000 = $197,040

Requisite rent per square foot:

$197,040 ÷ 30,000 sq. ft. = $6.57

Minimum rent:

30,000 sq. ft. × $6.57/sq. ft. = $197,040/yr. or $16,420/mo.

Calculating Percentage Rent

Percentage rent is a function of tenant sales productivity. Typically, a tenant's sales total during a lease year is multiplied by the percentage rent rate(s); any excess over the minimum rent is percentage rent.

Sales × % Rate − Minimum Rent = Percentage Rent

$1,100,000 × 6% = $66,000 − $60,000 = $6,000

Calculating the Breakpoint for Percentage Rent

The point at which tenants begin to pay percentage rent (the sales level at which they meet their minimum rent requirements) may be stipulated in leasing agreements in two ways:

- Natural breakpoints
- Unnatural breakpoints or artificial breakpoints

To calculate the natural breakpoint, managers use the formula:

$$\text{Breakpoint Sales} = \text{Minimum Rent} \div \% \text{ Rate}$$
$$\$1,000,000 = \$60,000 \div 6\%$$

Example: The minimum rent is $25,000 and the percentage rent rate is 5%. The natural breakpoint occurs when the tenant achieves $500,000 in sales.

$$\$500,000 = \$25,000 \div 5\%$$

An unnatural breakpoint is any designated breakpoint volume other than the natural one.

Example: A percentage rent is set at 6% on the first $300,000 of sales plus 5% on the excess above $300,000 (less, of course, the minimum rent). If the minimum rent is $25,000, the calculation of the unnatural breakpoint is:

Minimum rent	$25,000
Less the initial step ($300,000 × 6%)	− 18,000
	$ 7,000

Minimum rent at next step ($7,000 ÷ 5%)	$140,000

$300,000 in sales (initial breakpoint) + $140,000 in sales (second breakpoint) = $440,000 in sales (actual breakpoint)

Multiple Percentage Rates

Multiple percentage rates may be negotiated in the lease agreement. The percentage rent rate may vary by the category of sales (one rate for foodstuffs, another for liquor, etc.), or it may change at various increments of sales.

Example: A lease requires 6% of the first $300,000 in sales, plus 5% of the next $200,000, 4% of the next $100,000, and 3% of the excess above $600,000. If the minimum rent is $25,000 and sales amount to $800,000, the calculation of percentage rent is:

$300,000 × 6%	$18,000
$200,000 × 5%	10,000
$100,000 × 4%	4,000
$200,000 × 3%	6,000
	$38,000
Less the minimum rent	−25,000
Percentage rent (overage rent)	$13,000

Offsets

As part of lease negotiations, leases sometimes concede the offset of certain charges from the overage rent payment. The offsets may be the deduction of all or a portion of some expenses from all or a portion of overage rent.

Example: A lease allows the deduction of 50% of the common area charge. If the common area charge is $6,000, the tenant in the example above (where the overage rent earned was $13,000) can deduct $3,000. The net percentage rent plus common area charges payable would total $16,000. (This most commonly is recorded as $10,000 overage rent plus $6,000 common area charges, rather than $13,000 percentage rent plus $3,000 common area charge.)

Forecasting Percentage or Overage Rent

Overage rent (sometimes referred to percentage rent) is the amount of rent paid as a percentage of sales beyond the fixed minimum rent. However, some leases specify no minimum rents and therefore all rents are percentage rents—no overage rent. To forecast future income, start by examining existing rent rolls and tenant sales productivity. The managers' knowledge of market trends and tenant history come into play now as they predict tenants' changes in performance for the coming year. The budget may include various adjustments, including changes in percentage rent.

For appropriate and accurate timing of percentage rent income collection, it is important to realize two things about cash flow:

1. The projected periodic payments cannot be calculated by merely dividing the projected total into equal parts. Instead, calculate when the sales volumes are produced that trigger percentage rent.
2. As percentage rent is generated it is accrued until the end of a reporting period and is generally paid sometime in the following period.

Core Concepts

✓ Leased or leasable area
✓ Administrative fees

COMMON AREA EXPENSES

The recovery of common area expenses is another variable aspect of income management. Different tenants in a center may have different common area maintenance (CAM) rates; part of lease negotiation may be determining which formula to use to calculate the payment. Center management may not always recover all the costs.

Formulas

Following are the basic formulas for calculating common area expense recovery charges; the most commonly used is the fourth one (most tenants pay their share net of the anchors' share and net of the anchors' square footage).

1. Pro rata on leasable area
2. Pro rata on leased or occupied area
3. Pro rata on leasable area net of anchors' area and contributions
4. Pro rata on leased or occupied area net of anchors' areas and contributions
5. Flat rate per square foot
6. Zero
7. Fixed percentage of total costs
8. Percentage of sales

The above will vary by center type, however, as community centers usually include anchor stores in the denominator (#2). Many large retailers may also require that the anchor stores be added to the denominator, depending on the anchor definition in the lease. The lease is a negotiation, and terms can vary greatly from tenant to tenant.

Other Adjustments

Adjustments to the rates may include:

- Administrative markups
- Calculations based on the consumer price index (see below)
- Exclusions for specific tenants (for example, a bowling alley located on the periphery of a center might not pay for the mall's air conditioning)
- Limits and offsets for specific tenants

Example: If the landlord's common area cost, plus a 15% administrative markup, is prorated based on the ratio of a tenant's gross leasable area to leased GLA (net of department store GLA and net of department store contributions to common area cost), the calculation of the tenant's common area charge (using hypothetical numbers) is:

Total GLA	855,632 sq. ft.
Less vacant GLA	− 8,729 sq. ft.
Total leased GLA	846,903 sq. ft.
Less department store GLA	− 495,327 sq. ft.
Total non-department store leased GLA	351,576 sq. ft.
Landlord's common area cost	$2,327,562.00
Less department store contributions	− 955,327.00
Net common area cost	$1,372.235.00
Plus 15% markup	205,835.25
Total adjusted common area cost	$1,578,070.25
Total adjusted common area cost divided by total non-department store GLA	$4.49/sq. ft.
Tenant's GLA	3,179 sq. ft.
Tenant's pro rata share = (3,179 sq. ft. × $4.49/sq. ft.)	$14,273.71

Core Concepts

✓ Pro rata recovery
✓ Escalation
✓ Assessment

REAL ESTATE TAX RECOVERY

The calculations for real estate tax recovery charges are often similar to the CAM recovery formulas; the formula used to prorate tax payments is likewise negotiated as part of the lease agreement. The formulas include:

- Pro rata on leasable area
- Pro rata on leased or occupied area
- Pro rata on leasable area net of anchors' area and contributions
- Pro rata on leased or occupied area net of anchors' area and contributions
- Flat rate
- Escalation over base year(s)
- Current tax rate times initial assessment

- Pro rata of land portion tax plus tax rate times building assessment
- Taxes on expansion land or outparcels.

Tax calculations are usually more straightforward, as most tenants' realize that unlike CAM, the landlord does not control them. Many landlords hire consultants to deal with local assessors to keep the taxes under control. Some leases allow the landlord to recovery consultant's fees used to contest real estate tax assessments. Anchor tenants will usually attempt to have their parcel separately assessed.

Core Concepts

✓ CPI adjustments

CONSUMER PRICE INDEX ADJUSTMENTS

These adjustments use the federal government's published monthly consumer price index (CPIs) to determine the new rents. Existing leases will refer to which index was used at the time of agreement; that index becomes the lease's base index. The formula is the proportion:

$$\frac{\text{New rent}}{\text{Old rent}} = \frac{\text{Current CPI}}{\text{Base CPI}}$$

Example: If a $12-per-square-foot rent took effect in 1986, when the CPI was 109.6, what would the new rent be based on the CPI for January 1992, when the CPI was published at 138.1?

$$\frac{\text{New rent}}{\$12} = \frac{138.1}{109.6}$$

$$\text{New rent} = 138.1 \times \frac{12}{109.6} = \$15.12/\text{sq. ft.}$$

CPI increases may be applied to rents, marketing funds, or cam.

Core Concepts

✓ Specialty leasing income

OTHER SOURCES OF INCOME

A ll other income expected for the coming year must be included in the budget, including revenue generated from:

- Seasonal specialty leasing/temporary tenants
- Phone & vending income
- Fringe property, storage space, or lot rental
- Special events
- Parking charges
- Termination payments
- Late fees

Core Concepts

✓ Center value
✓ Tomorrow's dollars worth less
  than today
✓ ROI

CONCLUSION

A shopping center manager's job is to maximize the value of the center. To an investor, the critical element of a center's value is its earning power—the higher the anticipated earnings, the higher the value. Yet tomorrow's dollar will be worth less than today's, so interest rates are crucial in persuading investors to part with money and forgo its use elsewhere. Compound interest tables enable investors to compare the present and future value of money and calculate their return on investment (ROI). Analysis of the center's net cash flow leads to the capitalization rate that converts future income into current value. Due to the cap rate, even seemingly small improvements in a center's income stream can add dramatically to the center's value, so managers must attend to income and expenses. It is important to analyze the budget forecast and compare it with sales and rent levels. Financial analysis tools include monthly operating reports, cash flow statements, variance reports, and sales reports. Rents must be set to cover costs and the investor's desired ROI but are also influenced by the market. Minimum rent is supplemented by percentage rent. Lease negotiations may grant concessions to tenants, or allow for rent increases based on future productivity.

As with any position, the outline of your responsibilities will be your job description, filled in with rules, regulations, and sign-off limits that are part of the organization's policies and procedures. In the case of public companies, these are governed even further by the SEC regulations (such as with the Sarbanes Oxley Act). In the real estate industry, you will find a wide variance in what is expected of this position. The property manager's position requires a depth of knowledge regarding physical and operational aspects of the centers, as well as the financial ones. In smaller organizations, the manager may wear even more hats (construction coordination, marketing, etc.). Strong organizational skills are necessary to deal with the "multitasking" that frequently comes with managing shopping centers.

Appendix: Sample Shopping Center Appraisal Checklist

Location _____

Overall economy of trade area _____

Access and site considerations _____

Competition _____

Size of center (GLA) _____

Parking lot ratio _____

Land-to-building ratio _____

Position of anchor tenant _____

Tenant or merchandise mix _____

Quality of management _____

Store sizes _____

Lease dates and options _____

Percentage of space taken by major tenants ____

Participation in merchants' association _____

Quality of merchandise _____

Aesthetics, cleanliness, overall appeal _____

Safety and security _____

Percentage of income from minimum rents _____

Percentage of income from overage rents _____

Percentage of income from major tenants _____

Overage rents as a percentage of sales _____

Total sales per square foot _____

Participation in common area maintenance _____

Participation in real estate taxes _____

Total rent per square foot of minimum rents _____

Sales per square foot of each tenant _____

Trend of expenses _____

Expense-to-income ratio _____

Coverage of all expenses and debt service by guaranteed
    rents _____

Glossary

The glossary that follows is a listing of key definitions compiled from this outline, with several terms not defined in the outline added for your information. The terms are defined within the context of this shopping center management topic.

Accrued depreciation 1. The actual depreciation of a property at a given date; the difference between the cost of replacement new as of the date of appraisal and the present appraised market value. 2. In accounting, the amount reserved each year on the books of an owner to provide for the retirement and replacement of an asset.

Actual cash value The price that property will bring in a fair market, after fair and reasonable efforts have been made to find the purchaser who will give the highest price. Also called fair cash value. When used in context of insuring coverage, actual cash value means replacement cost less depreciation.

After-tax cash flow This is the cash throw-off less expenses and income tax liability. Taxable income will vary from year to year as mortgage interest payments and depreciation charges vary. These are deductions from cash throw-off to obtain taxable income. Income taxes themselves will vary accordingly. Thus, after-tax cash flow will be different each year by at least the tax differential caused by constantly declining interest deductions. Also called net spendable income.

Amortization The process of recovering, over a stated period of time, a capital investment; the provision for the gradual liquidation of an obligation, usually by equal payments at regular intervals over a specific period of time.

Breakpoint In percentage rent, the point at which rent due from a specific percentage of sales equals the minimum rent. See "Percentage rent."

CAM See "Common area maintenance."

Cap rate See "Capitalization rate."

Capital expense The annual amount required to pay interest on and provide for the ultimate return (depreciation or amortization) of the investment.

Capitalization The process of converting into a present value (obtaining the present worth of) a series of anticipated future annual installments of income.

Capitalization rate The rate used to convert income into value. Also known as cap rate.

Common area maintenance (CAM) The area maintained in common by all tenants, such as parking lots and common passages. This area is often defined in the lease and may or may not include all physical areas or be paid for by all tenants.

Compound interest The interest on interest; interest earned during a given period is added to the principal and included in the next period's interest calculation.

Consumer price index (CPI)   Various statistical indexes gathered and published by the federal government as economic indicators.

Cost approach   A method in which the value of a property is derived by estimating the replacement cost of the improvements, deducting the estimated depreciation, and adding the value of the land, as estimated by use of the market data approach.

Debt service   The payments consisting of amortization of and interest on a loan.

Depreciation   A loss from the upper limit of value caused by deterioration and/or obsolescence.

Discount rate   An interest rate commensurate with perceived risk; used to convert future payments or receipts to present value.

Equity   The net value of a property, obtained by subtracting from its total value all liens and other charges against it. The term is frequently applied to the value of the owner's (as opposed to the lender's) interest in property in excess of all claims and liens.

Gross leasable area (GLA)   The square footage of a shopping center that is designated for rental.

HVAC   Heating, ventilation, and air conditioning.

Income approach   An appraisal technique in which the anticipated net income is processed to indicate the capital amount of the investment that produces it. The capital amount, called the capitalized value, is, in effect, the sum of the anticipated annual rents less the loss of interest until the time of collection.

Interest   Money paid for the use of capital. It is usually expressed as a rate or percentage of the capital, called the interest rate.

Leverage   The use of borrowed funds to complete an investment transaction. The higher the proportion of borrowed funds used to make the investment, the higher the leverage and the lower the proportion of equity funds.

Market sales approach   An appraisal technique in which the market value estimate is predicated upon prices paid in actual market transactions and current listings. It is a process of correlation and analysis of similar recently sold properties. Also called the market data or comparable value approach.

Market value   The price expectable if a reasonable time is allowed to find a purchaser and if both seller and prospective buyer are fully informed. Market value connotes what a property is actually worth and market price what it might sell for.

Mortgage constant   The total annual payment of principal and interest (annual debt service) on a level-payment amortized mortgage, expressed as a percentage of the initial principal amount of the loan. It is used in mortgage-equity analysis as well as in estimating cash flows generated by income-producing real estate.

Multiple percentage rates A lease agreement in which the percentage rent rate changes at various increments of sales.

Net operating income The income after deducting from gross income the operating expenses, including property taxes, insurance, utilities, management fees, heating and cooling expense, repairs and maintenance, and replacement of equipment.

Offset A deduction of specified expenses or investments from all or a portion of percentage rent.

Operating expenses Generally speaking, all expenses, occurring periodically, that are necessary to produce net income before depreciation. Under some conditions these expenses are placed in two categories: operating expenses and fixed charges.

Overages Rent paid in addition to an agreed-upon minimum rent.

Percentage rent Percentage rent is a function of sales activity. A tenant's sales during a lease year are multiplied by the percentage rent rate(s); any excess over the minimum rent is overage rent.

Recapture rate The annual rate at which capital investment is returned to an investor over a specified period of time; the annual amount, apart from interest or return on interest (compound interest), that can be recaptured from an investment, divided by the original investment. Also called capital recovery rate.

Recovery rate The percentage of actual CAM and real estate taxes expense achieved or expected in a center during the year. (The CAM recovery rate for 2003 was 75%.)

Risk   The safety of the investment and the certainty of profitable yield in a given time.

Time value of money   The concept underlying compound interest: that a dollar received today is worth more than a dollar in the future, due to opportunity cost, inflation, and certainty of payment.

Value   The price an informed person is willing to pay on the open market.